P9-CMK-654

30°E 60° 90° 120° 150°

Arctic Ocean

A

I

ELAND

O P E

S

A

Pacific

Ocean

AFRICA

Indian

Ocean

AUSTRALIA

A N T A R C T I C A

Countries of the World

Ireland

Anna and Colm McQuinn

Elizabeth Malcolm and John McDonagh, Consultants

NATIONAL GEOGRAPHIC

WASHINGTON, D.C.

Contents

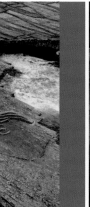

Foreword

reland is an ideal place to explore relationships among people, society, and environment. Lying northwest of continental Europe and separated from the island of Great Britain by the Irish Sea, it covers approximately 32,600 square miles (84,500 sq km) and has a population of a little over 6 million (4.3 million in the Republic; 1.74 million in Northern Ireland).

There are many Irelands. The first, and perhaps the most debated, is "divided" Ireland. The Republic of Ireland is made up of 26 counties and is a sovereign state. The remaining six counties make up Northern Ireland, part of the United Kingdom of Great Britain, and Northern Ireland. This division has a long history. It is not just a boundary in terms of territory. More significantly, the boundary created a divide in terms of community, where Catholics and Protestants lived in a constant state of tension and conflict. A great change has taken place recently. A peace process is now firmly in place following the signing of the Belfast Agreement, or Good Friday Agreement, in 1998.

Another Ireland is "tourist" Ireland, where images of rural life with thatched cottages, green fields, and friendly communities are marketed to visitors from Europe and the United States. There is the Ireland of "commerce and industry," where a modern, sophisticated, urban, and technologically advanced society that competes in the global marketplace takes center stage. There is "wealthy" Ireland. A country once overwhelmed by emigration and unemployment now has a new confidence and prosperity. The arrival of migrants from outside, full employment, and population growth are now normal. There is the "hidden" Ireland, where economic opportunity and modern lifestyles have fallen behind and where decline and exclusion continue in many

rural regions. There is the "new" Ireland, one that attempts to shrug off its conservative, religious, and rural image to embrace a more outward and cosmopolitan one. And a "contemporary" Ireland where there are struggles with new ideals, beliefs, and values and new challenges emerging from a growing multicultural and multiethnic society.

This book explores some of these issues through insights into the geography, history, politics, culture, and environment of Ireland and its people. Having packed such major change into the last fifteen years, the story of Ireland and where it travels to in the next decade will be intriguing to watch.

▲ Young girls perform a traditional Irish dance. Despite rapid economic progress, the Irish are eager to preserve their traditional culture.

John McDonagh
Department of Geography
University of Ireland, Galway

Forty Shades of Green

THE LUSH, GREEN FIELDS of Ireland have earned the country a famous nickname: the Emerald Isle. The fertile landscape results from a combination of Ireland's rich limestone soils and its wet but mild climate. Ireland is located on an island at the most westerly edge of Europe. The island is as far north as Labrador in Canada—but it is much less chilly. Ireland enjoys mild weather thanks to the Gulf Stream, a warming ocean current that arrives from Florida. The water around the island is warm enough to keep away icy weather systems from the Arctic.

Ireland has not always had a mild climate. During the last ice age, about 15,000 years ago, the country was covered in glaciers—sheets of ice that gouged out many of the landscape's more rugged features.

◀ A typical southern Irish patchwork of hedgerows and pastures rolls away beneath the Knockmealdown Mountains in Waterford County.

WHAT'S THE WEATHER LIKE?

Ireland's climate is influenced by the Atlantic Ocean. In summer, the ocean is cooler than the land, while in winter the water stays warm while the rocks and soil grow colder. As a result, the ocean ensures that Ireland never gets very hot or very cold.

If anything about Ireland's weather is extreme, it is the rainfall. The yearly total is not that high, but a rain shower is never far away. Most places get 40 inches (100 cm) of rain each year, and there is wet weather on 200 days of the year.

The map opposite shows the physical features of Ireland. Labels on this map and similar maps throughout this book identify most of the places pictured in each chapter.

Fast Facts

OFFICIAL NAME: Éire/Republic of Ireland
FORM OF GOVERNMENT: Constitutional Democracy
CAPITAL: Dublin
POPULATION: 4,109,086
OFFICIAL LANGUAGE: Irish/English
CURRENCY: Euro
AREA: 26,592 sq. miles (68,890 sq. km)
COASTLINE: 905 miles (1,448 km)
BORDERING NATIONS: United Kingdom
MAJOR MOUNTAIN RANGES: Macgillycuddy's Reeks, Wicklow Mountains
HIGHEST POINT: Carrantuohil 3,414 feet (1,041 m)
LOWEST POINT: Atlantic Ocean, sea level (0 feet)
MAJOR RIVERS: Shannon, Liffey, Boyne, Moy, Barrow
MAJOR LAKES: Lough Derg, Lough Corrib, Lough Mask

Average Temperature & Rainfall

Average High/Low Temperatures; Yearly Rainfall
CASTLEBAR (WEST):
55° F (13° C) / 41° F (5° C); 45 in (114 cm)
MULLINGAR (CENTER):
55° F (13° C) / 42° F (5° C); 38 in (96 cm)
DUBLIN (EAST):
55° F (13° C) / 43° F (6° C); 29 in (74 cm)
CORK (SOUTH):
55° F (13° C) / 43° F (6° C); 43 in (108 cm)

MAP KEY
Mild
☐ Marine West Coast

Irish Sea

Atlantic Ocean

0   mi   50
0   km   50

IRELAND
Europe
Asia
Atlantic
Ocean
Africa

Lough Swilly

North Channel

Bluestack Mts

Northern Ireland
(UNITED KINGDOM)

Donegal Bay

Mullet Peninsula

● Sligo

Ox Mountains

Moy

Shannon

Dundalk Bay

Achill Island

Clew Bay

Lough Conn

● Knock

● Drogheda

Boyne

Irish Sea

Lough Mask

C O N N A U G H T

Connemara

Lough Corrib

Lough Ree

I R E L A N D

Clare

MAN DIGGING IN BOG, page 11

ROCKY ISLAND, page 12

Galway ●

Galway Bay

Aran Islands

Grand

Canal

Liffey

⊛ Dublin

L E I N S T E R

Burren

Lough Derg

Wicklow Mountains

Cliffs of Moher

TALL CLIFFS, page 10

Shannon

**A t l a n t i c
O c e a n**

Nore

Barrow

Slaney

● Limerick

Golden Vale

RAINBOW OVER FIELDS, page 10

Mouth of the Shannon

Galty Mts

✛ *Rock of Cashel*

Suir

Comeragh Mts

Suir

Wexford ●

M U N S T E R

Knockmealdown Mountains

Waterford ●

St George's Channel

*Carrantuohill
(Highest point in Ireland)*
3,414 ft
✛ **+1,041 m**

Blackwater

GREEN FIELDS, pages 2, 6–7

Macgillycuddy's Reeks

Dingle Bay

Blarney ●

Lee

● Cork

Celtic Sea

Valentia Island

Bandon

COTTAGE BY THE SEA, page 13

FISHING BOAT IN HARBOR, page 13

MAP KEY

⊛ National capital

● Selected city

✛ Elevation

0   miles   50

0   km   50

Physical Map

▲ A rainbow hangs over the Golden Vale, a rich pastureland.

▼ The Cliffs of Moher rise 600 feet (180 m) above the Atlantic. They form the southern edge of the limestone Burren region.

An Island Called Ireland

There is often confusion about the land of Ireland because the name can apply to more than one place and country. The island of Ireland is the second-largest island in Europe. The other main island in this group is Great Britain to the east of Ireland. Ireland is divided between two countries. Just over 80 percent of the land makes up the Republic of Ireland, or Éire (pronounced air-uh). The other 20 percent in the northeast is Northern Ireland. This is part of the United Kingdom, along with England, Wales, and Scotland.

A Rich Landscape

The landscape of the Republic of Ireland is made up of lowland areas, which are mainly fields, surrounded by rocky hills and mountains. In many places, the land is

BOGS DOWN AND UP

Ireland has more bogs than any other country in Europe. About 15 percent of the country is covered by bogs, mostly in the midlands region or on the west coast. Bogs are damp areas filled with heavy soil called peat. They formed around 12,000 years ago after the last ice age. Glaciers melted, leaving behind many shallow lakes, which gradually filled with moss and dead wood. The water prevented this material from breaking down fully, and it has remained as peat ever since.

Ireland has two main types of bog—blanket bogs and raised bogs. Raised bogs form in low areas. They get their name because central areas bulge, or rise. Blanket bogs cover highland areas and are generally less common than raised bogs. However, Ireland has many of them—about 8 percent of the world's blanket bogs are in the country.

▲ A digger piles up blocks of peat cut from a bog. Until recently, peat was the main source of fuel in Ireland.

covered by damp peat bogs. The bogs and drier soils cover a bedrock of limestone. This rock helps to make Ireland's soils very fertile for growing crops and grass for cattle and sheep. One of the richest pastures is the Golden Vale, a large lowland spreading across the counties of Limerick, Tipperary, and Cork.

Exposed Stone

In some places the limestone bedrock comes above the surface. This is what happens in the Burren region located along the western coast in County Clare and County Galway. The Burren stretches over 140 square miles (360 square km). Much of the area has no soil,

The Aran Islands, on the west coast of Ireland, are almost solid rock—there is very little natural soil. The islanders traditionally grow their crops in soil made from seaweed, manure, and sand.

but is covered by a pavement of limestone. Plants grow in the cracks, or *grikes*, between the flat rocks, which are known as *clints*. In some places the limestone has been forced up by tectonic activity (gigantic underground forces) to a height of over 1,000 feet (300 m).

The Burren's limestone is up to 2,600 feet (800 m) thick in some parts. It was formed 340 million years ago when the area was at the bottom of a warm, shallow sea. Over the years, a deep layer of shells from dead corals, shellfish, and plankton built up on the seabed. These shells were gradually squeezed into solid rock. Over the years since, the Burren's rocks have been eaten away by ice and water, and there are many hundreds of small caves. With so much natural shelter around, the Burren has a long history of habitation. There are dozens of prehistoric stone buildings in the area.

Cliffs and Craggy Peaks

Ireland has some highland regions. Most of them are in the west and south and end with dramatic cliffs that plunge into the ocean. Just three Irish peaks are over 3,280 feet (1,000 m), all of which are in the Macgillycuddy's Reeks range in County Kerry in the far southwest.

CONNECTING CABLE

Valentia is a tiny island off the coast of County Kerry, best known for its slate. However, in 1865 it was put on the map for another reason. It became the starting point of the first transatlantic cable. The cable, which carried telegraph signals between Europe and North America, took nearly a year to lay. The largest ship in the world at the time, the SS *Great Eastern,* lowered hundreds of miles of cable to the ocean floor between Valentia and Newfoundland. Messages running through the cable were written down by operators stationed on the island. Another cable was used to forward signals to the mainland and on to anywhere in Europe.

▶ Valentia today is no longer at the center of world communications.

Island Slabs

The island of Valentia in Kerry's Dingle Bay is famous for its slate. The huge quarry has been working since 1816 and is now several miles across. The island's slate has been shipped around the world. It was used to tile the British parliament building in London, and it even ended up in the track beds of the San Salvador Railroad in Central America.

▼ Unsurprisingly for an island nation, the largest Irish cities are seaports. Here, a trawler is moored at a wharf in Cork, Ireland's second largest city.

In Touch
with
Nature

THE IRISH HAVE GREAT AFFECTION for nature and for rural life, and animals play a significant role in their legends and traditions. A sign of Ireland's link to the natural world is in its coins. Most countries put people on their money, such as kings or presidents. But the first Irish coins from the 1920s had animals on them. Some people objected to the decision. They thought that the coins should reflect Ireland's Christian religion, not older traditions.

The animals chosen were typical of Ireland's farms and countryside. For example, the penny had a chicken, and the sixpence had a wolfhound, an Irish dog breed. A salmon was on the two shilling coin, and a horse was on the half-crown. Ireland now uses the euro currency, so these coins are gone—but the close bond between the Irish and the natural world remains.

◀ **A farmer feeds a cow over an old stone wall on the Aran Islands.**

PROTECTING WILDLIFE

There are six national parks in Ireland. The largest ones cover the lakes and mountains of Killarney, Wicklow, and Donegal. A smaller national park protects a portion of the Burren, where two-thirds of Ireland's flower species grow.

Other parts of the country with important wildlife are designated as Natural Heritage Areas (NHA). For example, 75 raised bogs in the midland region are protected as NHAs. A further 73 blanket bogs, mostly in western areas, are also designated as NHAs. About 5,200 square miles (13,500 square km) form Special Areas of Conservation (SACs), which are protected by the European Union as well as the Irish authorities. The map opposite shows the main vegetation zones—what grows where in Ireland. Each zone is home to a distinct group of plants and animals.

▶ **A boggy lake is protected in the Connemara National Park.**

Species at Risk

Ireland is home to 28 species of land mammal, over 400 species of bird, more than 4,000 plant species, and more than 12,000 species of insect. Ireland has no history of polluting factories or expanding cities, at least until recent times. As a result most of the country's natural habitats have not been hugely damaged in the past. One exception are the peat bogs, which have been dug for fuel. Today, Irish wildlife is protected by government conservation programs. Species at risk include:

> basking shark
> common guitarfish
> common otter
> common porpoise
> Eurasian red squirrel
> European edible

> sea urchin
> European pond turtle
> freshwater pearl mussel
> white-clawed crayfish

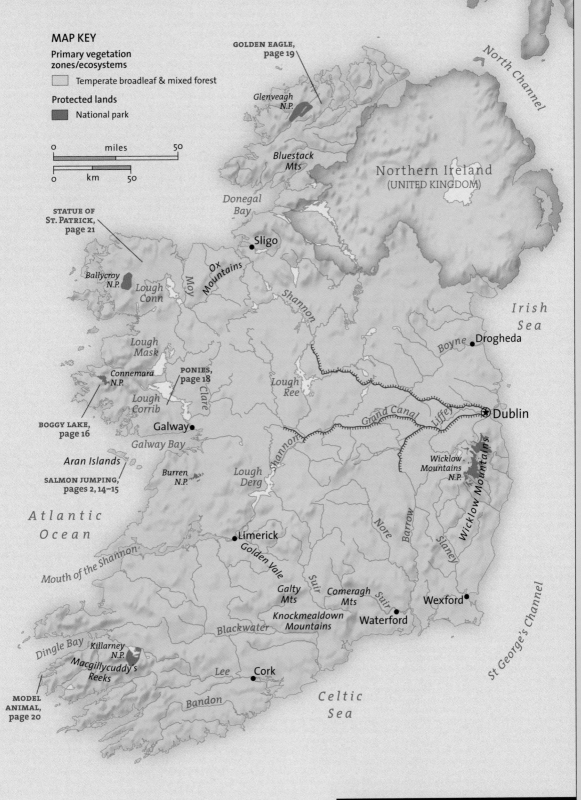

MAP KEY

Primary vegetation zones/ecosystems

Temperate broadleaf & mixed forest

Protected lands

National park

0   miles   50

0   km   50

GOLDEN EAGLE, page 19

Glenveagh N.P.

Bluestack Mts

Northern Ireland (UNITED KINGDOM)

North Channel

Donegal Bay

STATUE OF ST. PATRICK, page 21

Sligo

Ox Mountains

Moy

Irish Sea

Shannon

Ballycroy N.P.

Lough Conn

Boyne

Drogheda

Lough Mask

PONIES, page 18

Lough Ree

Connemara N.P.

Clare

Lough Corrib

Grand Canal

Liffey

BOGGY LAKE, page 16

Galway

⊛ Dublin

Galway Bay

Wicklow Mountains N.P.

Aran Islands

Burren N.P.

Lough Derg

Shannon

Wicklow Mountains

SALMON JUMPING, pages 2, 14–15

Atlantic Ocean

Nore

Barrow

Slaney

Limerick

Golden Vale

Suir

Comeragh Mts

Suir

Wexford

Mouth of the Shannon

Galty Mts

Knockmealdown Mountains

Waterford

St George's Channel

Blackwater

Dingle Bay

Killarney N.P.

Lee

Cork

MODEL ANIMAL, page 20

Macgillycuddy's Reeks

Bandon

Celtic Sea

Vegetation & Ecosystems Map

Horse-Crazy

The Irish love horses. It is not clear how or when horses came to Ireland, but archaeological excavations in the Boyne Valley show that horses played an important role in Ireland's earliest settlements.

Two breeds of horse have been identified as originating in Ireland. Bog ponies were bred for work in the peat industry. Peat was traditionally cut by hand. The bog was so muddy that small ponies were used to haul out the turf without sinking. Bog ponies grew only 40 inches (1 m) tall. They were also tough, so they did not panic if they got stuck in the mud. When tractors replaced ponies, the bog breed began to die out. There are now just 130 bog ponies in Ireland.

The second Irish breed is the Connemara pony from the west of County Galway. The history of this breed dates back to the time of the Celts 2,400 years ago. It is larger than a bog pony, standing about 52 inches (132 cm) tall; some are as tall as 58 inches (148 cm). The Connemara pony is strong and sturdy, with powerful back legs. It is a mixture of Andalusian and Arabian breeds. The ponies are tough but agile. They run and jump well, even over rough ground. The ponies get this ability from being bred for the rocky landscape of Connemara. The Connemara pony is the world's leading sports pony and is now bred all over the world for events such as show jumping.

Missing Animals

Because Ireland has been an island for thousands of years, the country does not have many animals. The surrounding sea has stopped species that are common elsewhere from reaching the land. For example, Ireland is famous for having no snakes. It has only two types of wild mouse, far fewer than most places. The

EAGLE RESCUE

The Republic of Ireland has the lowest number of birds of prey in Europe. During the last 100 years many species became extinct because of the destruction of their peat bog habitats. Today a number of projects aim to re-introduce hunting birds to Ireland.

In County Donegal, where there are a lot of blanket bogs suitable for eagles, golden eagle eggs were brought over from Scotland and placed in special cages. Once hatched, the chicks were fed through special openings to prevent any human contact. These birds are now living free as adults. In May 2007, golden eagle chicks hatched in a nest in Donegal for the first time in Ireland for almost a century.

▲ Golden eagles have been returned to Ireland by a conservation program.

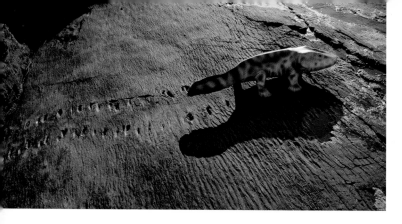

country also has just three types of amphibian: the common frog, the smooth newt, and the natterjack toad. This toad is found only in a few locations in County Kerry. It is more common in southern Europe and was possibly introduced to Ireland by humans in the last thousand years or so.

Although modern Ireland has few unusual animals, that was not always the case. In 1993 the footprints of an early land animal, called a tetrapod, were found in rocks on Valentia Island. The prints are 365 million years old and were made when the rock was still mud.

▲ Eddie, a model of a primitive animal about the size of a spaniel, shows how the fossil footprints were made on Valentia. Eddie was a relative of today's frogs and newts.

THE SALMON OF KNOWLEDGE

There are many stories about the hero Fionn mac Cumhaill and his band of warriors, the Fianna. The first one explains how he acquired the wisdom he used as a leader. As a boy, Fionn was the servant of a poet. For seven years, his master searched for a magic salmon called the Salmon of Knowledge. The fish had eaten nine hazelnuts that fell into the Well of Wisdom. In that way, the salmon gained all the knowledge in the world. The first person to eat any of it would gain this knowledge in turn.

The poet finally caught the salmon and asked his servant Fionn to cook it, warning him not to eat any. However, Fionn burned his thumb on the hot fish and sucked it to stop it from hurting. That was enough for the salmon's knowledge to pass to Fionn. From that day on, whenever Fionn needed to figure something out, he would put his thumb in his mouth.

▲ They say eating fish—especially the Salmon of Knowledge— is good for the brain.

PATRICK AND THE SNAKES

Ireland has no snakes (and only one type of lizard). This unusual situation is often explained by the legend of St. Patrick (*right*). The early Christian monk is said to have banished all snakes from the country.

A more scientific explanation is that snakes prefer a warm climate. They did not reach the British Isles from Europe until about 5,000 B.C., when Britain was warm enough. By then, the ice sheets had melted and the rising sea had surrounded Ireland. The new island was beyond the reach of snakes from Britain or Europe.

Giant Hound

There are several Irish breeds of dog, including the red setter, the water spaniel, and the Kerry blue terrier. The giant of them all is the Irish wolfhound. The wolfhound is one of the tallest dog breeds in the world, growing up to almost 3 feet (90 cm) in height. Despite the dog's size and strength, the wolfhound has a peaceful and quiet nature. Wolfhounds have excellent vision. They were bred to chase foxes over open ground. Wolfhounds make good pets because they are quiet indoors. However, they do require a lot of space, exercise—and food!

The wolfhound appears to be a very old breed. There is a record of it in Rome in A.D. 391, when Quintus Aurelius, the city's chief administrator, received seven wolfhounds as a gift. As with other animals, the wolfhound plays a part in many Irish legends.

▼ An Irish wolfhound towers above a terrier, another common dog in Ireland.

Comings
and
Goings

RELAND'S RICH HISTORY began sometime after 8000 B.C. when Stone Age people arrived from Spain, France, and the Middle East. They brought stone tools and they also knew how to farm crops for food. One of the world's oldest field systems still lies beneath a blanket of peat in County Mayo. In about 2500 B.C. copper and gold were introduced. Irish craftsmen made fine gold collars, necklaces, and earrings. The arrival of the Iron Age saw the emergence of the Celts. They are often referred to as the invisible people because they left no written records. The Celts paved the way for a last wave of Celts known as the Gaels. They arrived in Ireland in about 700 B.C. Their language may have started the Irish, or Gaelic, language that still exists today.

◄ The limestone walls of a cliff-top fortress can still be seen on the Aran Islands. This building was inhabited about 3,500 years ago.

ANCIENT CIVILIZATIONS

Archaeologists think that people reached Ireland about 6000 B.C. They lived on the coast and beside rivers, where they could fish, hunt, and gather fruits.

In about 3500 B.C., people began to use stone axes to clear forest for pastures and farmland. Some experts suggest that battles described between different groups in an 11th-century account called the *Book of Invasions* may reflect a conflict between Ireland's original hunter-gatherers and a new farming people. Archaeologists describe these new arrivals as neolithic—meaning the new Stone Age. Neolithic people built stone monuments, or cairns, as tombs and for ceremonies.

▲ **The Uragh stone circle in County Kerry was built about 4,000 years ago by a neolithic community.**

In about 1800 B.C. metalworkers came to Ireland, attracted by its supply of copper. They mixed copper from Ireland with tin from Spain to make bronze, and beat Irish gold into moon-shaped necklaces and other ornaments. When the Celtic people arrived in 700 B.C., according to legend, they could not conquer the Tuatha Dé Danann, people said to make magical metal objects. So the Celts gave the Tuatha the underworld. The Tuatha became the "fairy people" of Irish legend.

Time line

This chart shows the approximate dates of events in the history of Ireland from A.D. **200** to the present day.

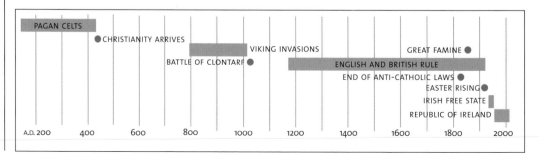

PAGAN CELTS

● CHRISTIANITY ARRIVES

VIKING INVASIONS

GREAT FAMINE ●

BATTLE OF CLONTARF ●

ENGLISH AND BRITISH RULE

END OF ANTI-CATHOLIC LAWS ●

EASTER RISING ●

IRISH FREE STATE

REPUBLIC OF IRELAND

A.D. 200   400   600   800   1000   1200   1400   1600   1800   2000

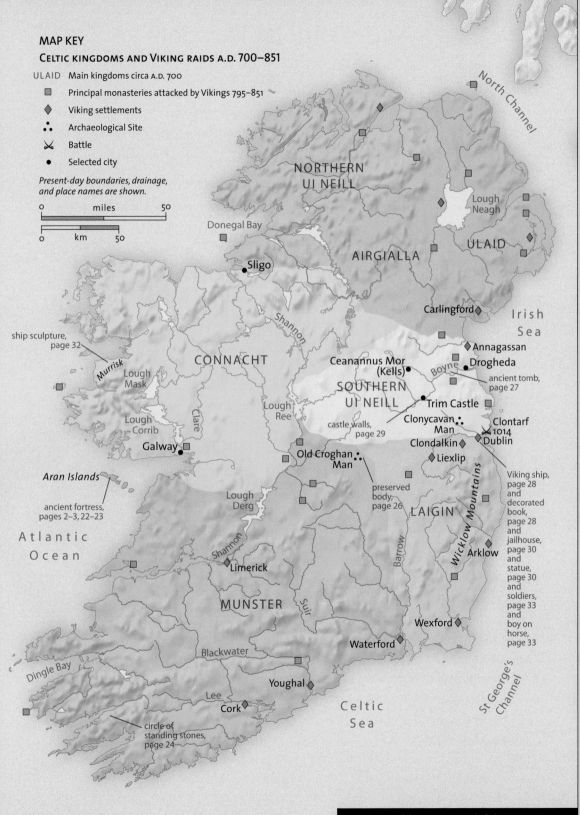

MAP KEY

CELTIC KINGDOMS AND VIKING RAIDS A.D. 700–851

ULAID   Main kingdoms circa A.D. 700

▪   Principal monasteries attacked by Vikings 795–851

◆   Viking settlements

∴   Archaeological Site

✕   Battle

●   Selected city

Present-day boundaries, drainage, and place names are shown.

0   miles   50

0   km   50

North Channel

NORTHERN UI NEILL

Lough Neagh

ULAID

AIRGIALLA

Donegal Bay

Sligo

Irish Sea

Carlingford

ship sculpture, page 32

Murrisk

Lough Mask

CONNACHT

Shannon

Ceanannus Mor (Kells)

Boyne

Annagassan

Drogheda

ancient tomb, page 27

Lough Corrib

Lough Ree

SOUTHERN UI NEILL

Trim Castle

Clonycavan Man

Clontarf 1014

Dublin

Galway

castle walls, page 29

Old Croghan Man

Clondalkin

Liexlip

Aran Islands

ancient fortress, pages 2–3, 22–23

Clare

Lough Derg

preserved body, page 26

LAIGIN

Wicklow Mountains

Viking ship, page 28 and decorated book, page 28 and jailhouse, page 30 and statue, page 30 and soldiers, page 33 and boy on horse, page 33

Atlantic Ocean

Shannon

Limerick

Suir

Barrow

Arklow

MUNSTER

Wexford

Waterford

St George's Channel

Blackwater

Youghal

Lee

Cork

circle of standing stones, page 24

Dingle Bay

Celtic Sea

Superstitious Warriors

Some experts believe that a powerful force of Celts, originally from central Europe, arrived in Ireland in 700 B.C., probably via Spain. The Celts knew how to work iron. Their iron weapons were superior to the bronze arms of the people then living in Ireland. Celtic, or Gaelic, culture became dominant throughout the island. The earlier people were not wiped out completely, however. Some experts even argue that there was no great arrival of Celts. They say that local people adopted Celtic ideas and language.

In traditional history, the Celts were in awe of the original Irish—the Tuatha Dé Danann, who feature in Irish myths. The newcomers did not destroy the ancient cairns, or mounds of stones, in case it disturbed the

BOG BODIES

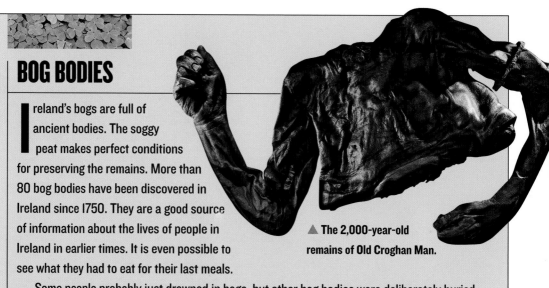

Ireland's bogs are full of ancient bodies. The soggy peat makes perfect conditions for preserving the remains. More than 80 bog bodies have been discovered in Ireland since 1750. They are a good source of information about the lives of people in Ireland in earlier times. It is even possible to see what they had to eat for their last meals.

▲ The 2,000-year-old remains of Old Croghan Man.

Some people probably just drowned in bogs, but other bog bodies were deliberately buried. Old Croghan Man, who was found in 2003 in central Ireland, was a human sacrifice. At 6.5 feet (196 cm) tall, he would have been a giant by ancient standards and made a powerful offering to the gods. Bog bodies are so well preserved that even hairstyles are still intact. Clonycavan Man, who was thrown into a bog 2,300 years ago, used hair gel made from pine resin to make his hair stand up. He was just 5 feet 2 inches (157 cm) tall, so perhaps he wanted to look a little taller.

LIGHTING THE WAY

The passage tombs of Newgrange, Knowth, and Dowth lie in the Boyne Valley near the east coast of Ireland. They were built around 3200 B.C., making them older than the Pyramids of Giza in Egypt. They were built by farming peoples as a place to bury important leaders and also for holding religious ceremonies. Many of the ceremonies marked changes in the seasons. For example, on the morning of the winter solstice (the shortest day of the year), the rising sun shines into the entrance of the Newgrange tomb through a perfectly aligned hole. Gradually the sunlight moves down the passage, lighting up the tomb.

▲ A carved stone stands at the entrance to the Newgrange tomb.

magical "little people" or fairies. This respect for ancient sites lasted in Ireland for a long time, but some sites are now threatened by development.

The Iron-Age Irish lived in family groups in circular forts. Some were stone but most were earth banks, probably topped with a wooden fence. There are some 30,000 of these "fairy forts" in Ireland.

▼ The so-called Celtic Cross mixes old pagan designs and carvings with the Christian cross.

Becoming Christian

In the fifth century A.D. Ireland became a Christian country. According to tradition, the religion arrived with St. Patrick in A.D. 432, who spent 30 years preaching in Ireland. Irish monks lived in monasteries, each one with a church, library, and workshop. The monks each had a small bedroom called a cell. Irish monasteries became centers of learning, crafts, and politics.

After the Roman Empire collapsed in the sixth century, Ireland's Christians became isolated. The religion continued to grow there, while other areas of Europe were overrun by pagan peoples. Ireland became known as a land of saints and scholars. People went there to study, and Irish monks spread Christianity across Europe.

Viking Plunderers

The wealth of Ireland's monastery communities attracted a new wave of invaders—Vikings from Scandinavia. In the ninth century, Vikings attacked Irish

THE BOOK OF KELLS

The Book of Kells is a copy of the Christian gospels made around A.D. 800. The book is named for the town of Kells, north of Dublin, where it was kept from the 11th century on. However, it is possible that the book originated in Scotland or even northern England. It is written in Latin on vellum—tough paper made from calfskin. The text is illustrated with many intricate color pictures. The original manuscript was given to Trinity College, Dublin, in the 17th century. It is now on display in the college's Old Library.

▲ St. Matthew pictured in the Book of Kells.

coastal settlements. The raiders did not just plunder, however. They also set up trading posts. Most of Ireland's modern cities, including Dublin (the capital), Wicklow, Wexford, Waterford, Cork, and Limerick, began as Viking settlements. The Vikings and Celts clashed often over the next 200 years, but gradually the two communities merged. Peace was finally achieved when the great Irish king, Brian Boru, united most of the country at the Battle of Clontarf in 1014. However, just as Brian Boru gave thanks for the victory in his tent, he was killed by a retreating Viking.

Norman Invasion

Ireland once again broke into several small warring kingdoms. One leader, Dermot MacMurrough, went to England to ask the Normans to help him win territory in Ireland. The Normans were Vikings (or Norsemen) who had recently invaded England from France.

Dermot made an alliance with a Norman lord named Strongbow, who brought an army to Ireland in 1170. The Normans captured Waterford and Dublin easily. Their successes attracted the English king, Henry II. He was worried that Strongbow would make

▼ Trim Castle was built by Normans beside the Boyne River in County Meath. Today it remains the largest Norman castle in the world.

himself lord of Ireland. However, Strongbow swore loyalty to Henry, who took control of a large Irish territory, called a lordship.

English Control

Over the years, the Normans lost their lands in France and became purely English rulers. They also began to lose territory in Ireland and built castles to defend the most important places. By the 1500s the English only controlled Dublin and a few other ports, and it looked like they would soon lose them, too. Over the next century English armies were sent to take back land, and by 1603 they had conquered the whole island.

At the same time, England was changing from a Roman Catholic country to a Protestant one. However, most Irish people were Catholics, and Protestant lords took away much of their land. That caused a rift that remained in Ireland for many decades.

Controlling Laws

Catholics—especially in Ireland—were seen as a threat to the British crown (England, Wales, Scotland, and Ireland had now joined to become Great Britain). In the 17th century new laws were created to keep control. Catholics were banned from practicing their religion, and speaking Irish was made illegal. Catholics were not allowed to join the British parliament, the

THE IRISH ABROAD

▲ Proud Irish Americans take part in Chicago's St. Patrick's Day parade dressed in emerald green. Patrick is Ireland's main saint.

For much of its history, Ireland has been a land of emigrants. Today, people of Irish descent live mainly in Britain, North America, and Australia. Most people left Ireland only because they had to. The largest wave of emigration began during the famine of the late 1840s. By 1911 the population had fallen by half, from 8 to 4 million.

The emigrants made sure that they did not forget their culture. They often exaggerated a little when telling their children about a beautiful green land with a rich history and culture.

The Irish were not always welcome in their new lands and found themselves having to struggle against injustice. Many entered politics. A third of U.S. presidents have had Irish ancestors, including John Kennedy and Bill Clinton. Irish names also appear in Latin American politics. Bernardo O'Higgins was the first president of Chile. Patricio Lynch ruled Peru. Che Guevara, the 1950s communist rebel, was also from the Lynch family. His father, Ernesto Guevara Lynch, said: "My son's veins flowed with the blood of Irish rebels."

armed forces, or work for the government or as a lawyer. They could not run schools, own houses, or buy land. An elder son could only inherit all of his father's land if he became a Protestant. Instead, Irish farms were divided between several sons and became ever smaller. By 1776, 80 percent of the Irish were Catholic, but they owned just 5 percent of the land.

Liberation, then Disaster

A mass movement against anti-Catholic laws reached its height in the 1820s. It was led by Daniel O'Connell, who organized huge, peaceful demonstrations. The discriminating laws were finally overturned in 1829.

▲ The *Coffin Ship* sculpture in Murrisk is the national monument to the Great Famine.

Less than two decades later, Ireland was shattered by its worst disaster—the Great Famine. Much of the food grown on Irish farms was sold abroad, and farmworkers were not paid. Instead they were given land to grow their own food. Most plots were only big enough to grow potatoes.

In 1846, a fungus called potato blight killed most of the crop. Families went hungry. By 1851 a million people had died of starvation or disease. A further million fled to Britain and the Americas. The journey was wretched—the ships were overcrowded and full of disease. On some trips as many as half the passengers died. People called the vessels "coffin ships."

Republican Rising

Despite small improvements in the way Ireland was ruled from London, the calls for Ireland to govern itself continued to grow. The Irish Republican Brotherhood (IRB) became influential. The IRB were also known as the Fenians, a name from the *Fianna*, a band of heroes in Irish legends. The IRB were involved in many violent revolts, the largest being the Easter Rising of 1916. On Easter Monday that year, armed Fenians occupied several buildings in Dublin. British troops ended the rising in a few days, but their violence increased support for a complete break with Britain. In 1919, the Irish Republican Army (IRA) was formed. A bloody guerilla war began across the country between the IRA and the British authorities. In 1921 the two sides called a truce and peace talks began.

The Irish Free State

A treaty created the Irish Free State in 1922. The new country was ruled from Dublin but was still part of the British Empire. Irish citizens had to swear loyalty to the British king. In addition, the state only included 26 of the 32 Irish counties. Six counties in the northeast were home to mainly Protestant populations. They remained under British rule as the province of Northern Ireland.

Over the next 25 years, the Irish Free State slowly loosened its ties with Britain. It stayed neutral during World War II. In 1948 it made a total break with Britain and became a republic. The Republic of Ireland (Éire in Irish) remained a nation of farmers with little industry. Many of its people still had to leave to find work abroad. However, rapid change in the 1990s improved the economy. The Irish are now the fifth-wealthiest people on Earth.

▲ British soldiers take cover behind beer barrels on a Dublin harborside during the Easter Rising.

▼ A boy rides bareback past an apartment building near Dublin. Until the 1990s Ireland was a relatively poor country.

Tradition
and
Change

RELAND'S MIX OF TRADITIONS and culture is celebrated in many stories and poems. Thanks to an economic boom in recent years, however, the country is changing quickly. Traditional practices have been replaced by modern attitudes and industry. Despite the rapid change, land, religion (nearly 90 percent of the Irish are Roman Catholics) and politics are still vital to much of life in Ireland.

The Irish have a strong bond with their landscape. That bond shapes their attitude about preserving ancient sites, often out of a belief that destroying them will bring bad luck. As a result, Irish culture is based on history. The past is very much part of the present, from neolithic tombs to monasteries and castles. People also remember the long history of Irish rebellion.

◄ The Ha'penny Bridge carries a footpath over the River Liffey in Dublin. It is a much loved landmark and a link to the past in a city that is rapidly modernizing.

NEW ARRIVALS

As the Irish economy has grown in the last decade, the country has seen huge changes. Cities have swelled with people and once quiet towns have become busy with commuters.

For the first time since the 1840s, the population is rising. The rise is due to returning Irish emigrants and foreigners seeking work. Most immigrants are English, Polish, Chinese, or Nigerian. The Irish are used to living abroad, but today they must adjust to welcoming foreigners to their own country.

Common Irish Phrases

Most Irish people speak English, but some also speak a separate language, called Irish, or Gaelic. Several Irish words are used by Ireland's English speakers, often as slang. Give them a try:

Good luck	Sláinte (slaw-in-chuh)
A good time	Craic (crack)
A city person	Jackeen
A country person	Culchie
Idiot (man)	Eejit
Idiot (woman)	Ónseach (own shuck)

Irish people are very friendly. They often say "Thanks a million" when you do something nice for them. This comes from the Irish "Go raibh míle maith agat," which means "May you have a thousand good things happen to you."

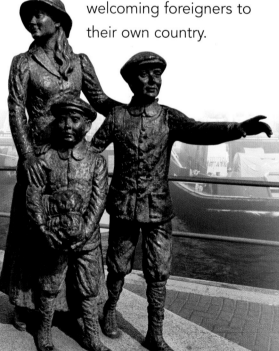

◀ A statue of 19th-century Irish emigrants looks out toward America from Cobh, County Cork. Today people do not leave Ireland in such large numbers; many foreigners are instead choosing to live there.

1950 / 2.97 million	1970 / 2.95 million
41% urban — 59% rural	51% urban — 49% rural

1990 / 3.51 million	2005 / 4.15 million
56% urban — 44% rural	60% Urban — 40% rural

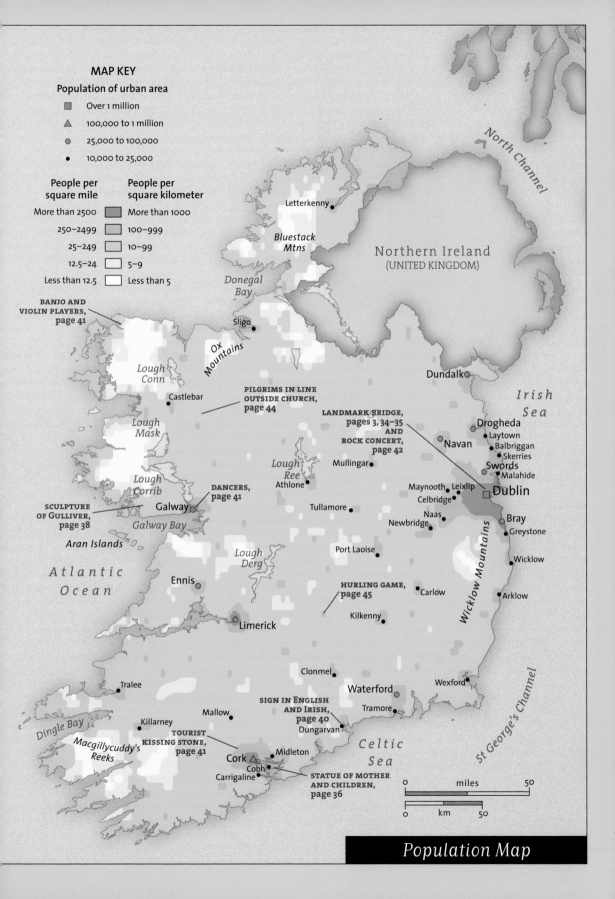

MAP KEY

Population of urban area

■ Over 1 million

▲ 100,000 to 1 million

● 25,000 to 100,000

• 10,000 to 25,000

People per square mile	People per square kilometer
More than 2500	More than 1000
250–2499	100–999
25–249	10–99
12.5–24	5–9
Less than 12.5	Less than 5

North Channel

BANJO AND VIOLIN PLAYERS, page 41

Letterkenny

Bluestack Mtns

Northern Ireland (UNITED KINGDOM)

Donegal Bay

Sligo

Ox Mountains

Irish Sea

Dundalk

Lough Conn

Castlebar

PILGRIMS IN LINE OUTSIDE CHURCH, page 44

LANDMARK BRIDGE, pages 3, 34–35 AND ROCK CONCERT, page 42

Drogheda
Laytown
Balbriggan
Skerries

Lough Mask

Navan

Mullingar

Swords
Malahide

Lough Ree

Athlone

Maynooth
Leixlip

Dublin

Lough Corrib

DANCERS, page 41

Galway

Tullamore

Celbridge

SCULPTURE OF GULLIVER, page 38

Galway Bay

Naas

Bray

Greystone

Aran Islands

Lough Derg

Newbridge

Port Laoise

Wicklow

Atlantic Ocean

Ennis

Carlow

HURLING GAME, page 45

Arklow

Wicklow Mountains

Limerick

Kilkenny

Tralee

Clonmel

Wexford

SIGN IN ENGLISH AND IRISH, page 40

Waterford

Mallow

Tramore

St George's Channel

Killarney

TOURIST KISSING STONE, page 41

Dungarvan

Celtic Sea

Macgillycuddy's Reeks

Dingle Bay

Midleton

Cork

Cobh

Carrigaline

STATUE OF MOTHER AND CHILDREN, page 36

0	miles	50

| 0 | km | 50 |

A Nation of Storytellers

Irish people have always loved stories. This tradition is a long one. Celtic bards were poets, storytellers, priests, and lawyers mixed into one. It was their job to record the history of Ireland. They recited and sang stories while playing the lyre or harp. Bards were very powerful. Everyone had to be respectful toward them—they could spread bad gossip about a person otherwise.

▲ A nun stands by a sculpture of Gulliver on a beach in Galway. On his travels, by Irish writer Jonathan Swift, Gulliver is washed up in Lilliput, a land of tiny people.

Bards had disappeared by the 1600s, but the Irish have continued their love affair with stories. Four Irish writers have won a Nobel prize for literature: W. B. Yeats (1923), George Bernard Shaw (1925), Samuel Beckett (1969), and Seamus Heaney (1995). Stories

FOWL READING

Eoin (pronounced Owen) Colfer is one of the most successful Irish writers working today. He was born in Wexford on the southeast coast of Ireland in 1965. He first became interested in writing after hearing gripping stories about Vikings in history lessons.

Colfer writes for children, and he is famous for the Artemis Fowl fantasy series. Artemis Fowl is an Irish criminal mastermind, with a difference—he is a teenager, and he has set his sights on stealing fairy gold. The only thing that stands between Fowl and his prize is a special unit of the fairy police. These are not normal leprechauns from Irish myths, but the highly trained LEP Recon squad.

▲ Eoin Colfer has written seven *Artemis Fowl* books.

HIGHLY STRUNG

The harp is an important symbol of Ireland. Stone carvings of harps from the 10th century show that the instrument has been played in Ireland for at least 1,000 years. According to myth, the first harp was owned by Dagda, a chief of Tuatha Dé Danaan, the metalworkers of prehistory. This has a ring of truth, because Celtic harps were traditionally strung with metal wires. A harp on display in Trinity College, Dublin, is said to have belonged to Brian Boru, the heroic king of 10th-century Ireland. Although it actually dates from the 14th century, Brian Boru's harp appears on Irish coins, including the euros now used in the country.

▲ A girl gets a harp lesson.

written by other Irish authors are also famous, such as *Dracula* by Bram Stoker and *Gulliver's Travels* by Jonathan Swift. James Joyce wrote several famous, although hard to read, novels, including *Ulysses*.

Irish or English?

Much of Irish literature in the past was written in the Irish, or Gaelic, language. Gaelic is the oldest written script in Europe after Greek and Latin. Nowadays, however, almost all of Irish writing is in English. About 14 percent of the population can read Irish, and only 30,000 people—less than 1 percent of the population—speak Irish as a first language.

The version of English spoken in Ireland, however, is unique. If you listen to Irish people speak, you might think that only the accent and some words are different.

In fact, the whole construction of the language is different. Linguists call the Irish dialect (form of language) Hiberno-English. It is unique because Irish people still use Irish grammar to construct English sentences. For example, there is no word for "yes" or "no" in Irish. You can test this by asking an Irish person "Are you Irish?" In Irish, they will answer "I am" rather than "yes." In English, some Irish people will also say "I am."

▲ A road sign in Ireland is written in both English and Irish.

Loaning Words

The Irish language has given many words to English. These are called "loan words"—but they're here to stay! *Whiskey* may be the most famous. This word comes from the Irish phrase *uisce beatha*, meaning "water of life." Another loan word is *phoney*, which comes from Irish immigrants selling fake gold rings, or *fáine*. The word *boycott* is not an Irish language word but a man's name. Charles Boycott was a landlord who charged very high rents. His tenants refused to pay, and now this same sort of protest is called a boycott.

Oscar Wilde, an Irish writer, said that the Irish are the greatest talkers since the Greeks, so it is no surprise that they have also given the world words for talking. If you have the "gift of the gab," it means you are a good talker. The phrase comes from *gob*, the Irish word for "mouth." What the Irish actually say is described as "blarney." This comes from Lord Blarney, an Irish chieftain of the 1500s. He was asked to declare his loyalty to the English queen, Elizabeth I. He gave such a long, complicated answer that nobody could work out whether he was for or against her! Many tourists kiss the Blarney Stone at the earl's castle in the hope of gaining the "gift of the gab."

Making Music

Irish music has its roots in ancient Celtic culture. *Sean-nós*, or "old style," Irish songs are traditionally sung by several people without musical instruments. Other types of Irish music are meant for dancing. They are played with pipes, harps, and other stringed instruments, such as banjos and violins. Dancers, generally in sets of four couples, dance a series of steps. Each set of steps has a name, such as Ladies' Chain or The High Gates. Each dance is suited to a type of tune, such as reels, jigs, and polkas. There is a pause between each dance for the dancers to catch their breath.

Irish stepdancing is more of a solo dance form, although a form performed by large groups of

▲ A visitor kisses the Blarney Stone, which is said to make people very skilled speakers.

▼ Local musicians play traditional music in a bar in County Mayo.

▲ The performances in the *Riverdance* show are based on Irish dance.

dancers was popularized across the world by the success of the 1990s Broadway musicals *Riverdance* and *Lord of the Dance*.

Modern Rockers

Traditional Irish music has a large following around the world through recording artists such as the Chieftains. Its influence can be heard in bluegrass and other American roots-music styles. However, the country's musicians have also been influenced by musical styles from abroad. In the 1970s Ireland produced its own brand of pop and rock music, with Van Morrison and Thin Lizzy.

▼ U2 gives a hi-tech performance in their hometown of Dublin.

HIGH-TECH MUSIC

Many Irish musicians have embraced new technologies to merge old and new sounds. Among the most successful is Enya (*right*), who combines traditional Celtic melodies with ethereal electronic sounds. Enya has composed songs for movies such as *Lord of the Rings* and *Far and Away*. In 2006, another Irish singer, Majella Murphy, made history when she became the first artist to launch an album to be downloaded and played on cell phones.

The biggest Irish musical success is U2, a 1980s rock band, which continues to sell millions of records around the world. The most successful Irish bands of recent times are the Corrs and Westlife.

The U2 singer, Bono, is also an international charity campaigner, along with Bob Geldof, another Irish-born musician. Geldof had some musical success in the early 1980s, but is now more famous for his work organizing the global charity concerts Live Aid and Live 8.

Sports and Luck

Like people the world over, the Irish are big sports fans. They have top national teams in rugby and soccer, and have produced several world-class golfers. Horse racing is also a hugely popular spectator sport, with many people making bets on the winners. Horses bred in Ireland win races throughout the world.

NATIONAL HOLIDAYS

Unlike most countries, Ireland has few holidays celebrating national events. There are four holidays each year that give people a three-day weekend. People also take days off work at Christmas, New Year's, and Easter. The other important days are Catholic saints' days. St. Patrick's Day is a public holiday, but most saints' days are not official holidays. In July, thousands of Irish people make a pilgrimage to Knock, County Mayo, to attend the church (above) where a miracle was said to have occurred in 1879.

NEW YEAR'S DAY	January 1
ST. PATRICK'S DAY	March 17
EASTER	moveable
LABOUR DAY/MAY DAY	first Monday in May
JUNE HOLIDAY	first Monday in June
AUGUST HOLIDAY	first Monday in August
OCTOBER HOLIDAY	last Monday in October
CHRISTMAS DAY	December 25
ST. STEPHEN'S DAY	December 26

High-Speed Games

There are also a number of sports played only in Ireland. Hurling is the oldest and one of the most popular ones. It has been played since the start of recorded history in Ireland 1,500 years ago. A few fragments of a document from about A.D. 400 are thought to contain some of the rules of hurling.

The game may be the world's fastest field sport. The ball can travel at up to 100 miles per hour (160 kmh). Players use a wooden stick called a hurley, which is a little like a hockey stick, to hit or carry a small ball. They can also kick the ball or slap it with their open hand. Players can catch the ball and carry it for up to four steps. A player who wants to carry the ball farther has to bounce or balance the ball on the end of the stick.

Players score by hitting the ball between H-shaped goalposts at either end of the field. A ball over the crossbar

RUNNING WITH THE BALL

Gaelic football is the most-played sport in Ireland, where it was first recorded in 1527. The sport has similarities with soccer and rugby. There are 15 players on each team, and they kick and carry the ball around the field. Gaelic football has its own techniques, however. In "fielding," players jump against each other to catch the ball. "Soloing" is a technique where a player repeatedly kicks and catches the ball while running along. The game uses the same H-shaped goalposts as hurling. One point is scored when the ball goes over the crossbar; three points are scored when the ball goes into the net.

▲ Gaelic football tackles are made with one arm.

scores one point; under the crossbar into the net guarded by a goalkeeper scores three points.

The women's equivalent of hurling is called *camogie*. Its rules are identical to hurling except women can also score with their hands. Hurling is an amateur sport. No one gets paid for playing hurling, even though the All-Ireland Senior Hurling Final is watched in Dublin by more than 70,000 fans.

▼ Players from the Cork and Tipperary teams race for the ball during a big hurling match.

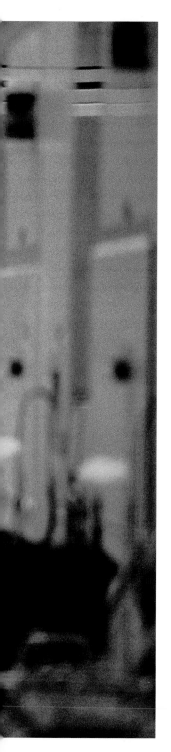

Changing Fortunes

WITH FEW NATURAL RESOURCES, the Irish economy was dominated by agriculture for most of the country's history. Even after World War II (1939–1945), when many countries were busy building factories, the Irish did not. Being an island made it expensive to import the raw materials needed for large-scale industry and even more expensive to export finished products.

In addition to such practical problems, when Ireland became independent, many Irish had a vision of a self-sufficient nation—a land where farmers on small farms lived simple lives. But a few decades later Ireland's economy was failing. The government had to change direction. Its plan worked, and today Ireland is one of the wealthiest countries in the world.

◀ **Technicians work in an ultra-modern microchip factory near Dublin. Many large companies have set up businesses in Ireland in the last 20 years.**

Government & Economy   **47**

GETTING REPRESENTED

Ireland is divided into voting areas, known as constituencies. Each area elects at least three Teachtá Dálas (TDs—members of parliament), but some have as many as five. There must be at least one TD for every 30,000 people. There are currently 166 TDs representing 41 constituencies.

Irish electors vote for parties rather than particular people. Each political party puts up three candidates for every constituency, more in larger areas, ranked in order. Once a party gets above a certain proportion of the total votes cast, its top-ranked candidate is elected. The rest of the party's votes are moved to the next candidate on the list, and so on. This voting system is called proportional representation. It ensures that parties get a fair proportion of seats.

► **The dome of Leinster House, the Irish parliament building, is lit up at night.**

Trading Partners

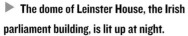

Ireland's largest trading partners are its eastern and western neighbors—the United Kingdom and the United States. Almost a third of imports arrive via a short voyage across the Irish Sea from Britain. Ireland imports its fuel and high-tech machinery and electronics. The largest export partner is the United States; exports include pharmaceuticals (medicines) and food.

Country	Percent Ireland exports
United States	19.7%
United Kingdom	17.7%
Belgium	14.7%
Germany	7.7%
All others combined	40.2%

Country	Percent Ireland imports
United Kingdom	30.7%
United States	13.9%
Germany	7.5%
China	5.7%
All others combined	42.2%

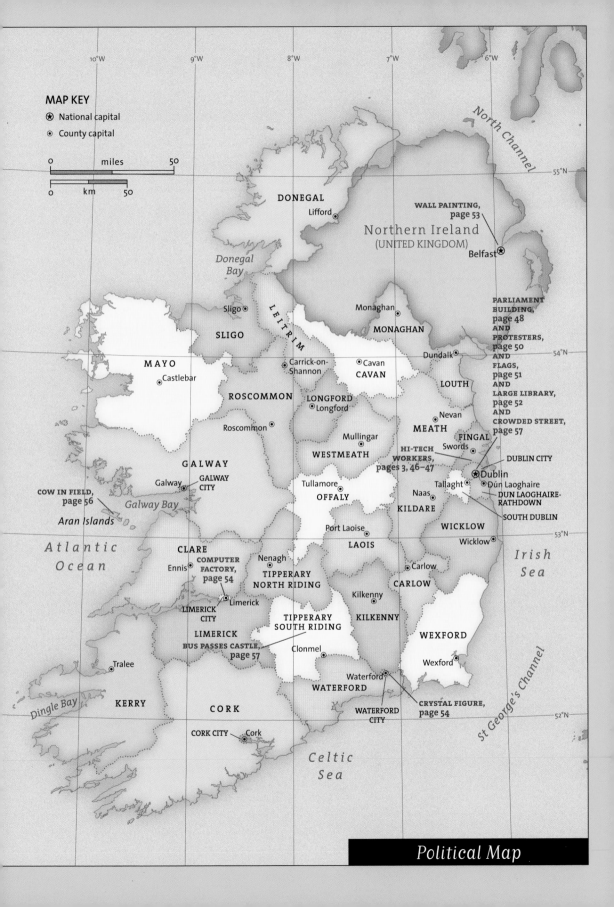

Having A Say

Modern Ireland is a highly democratic country. As well as electing representatives to the Dáil (parliament) and a president at regular intervals, the Irish are also asked to vote on certain important issues. These public votes are known as referenda. The Irish constitution says that changes to the way Ireland is governed must be approved by a referendum. For example, Ireland's entry into the

▲ Campaigners hold signs urging voters to keep divorce illegal in a public vote in 1997.

HOW THE GOVERNMENT WORKS

Ireland is a parliamentary democracy. All citizens over 18 have the right to vote in elections. Laws are passed by the Irish parliament, or Oireachtas. This consists of two houses. Elected TDs sit in the Dáil Éireann (House of Representatives). The members of the Seanad Eireann (Senate) are either elected or appointed. An election to the Dáil is held every five years.

The head of the government is called the Taoiseach (pronounced tee-shuck, literally meaning "chief"). He or she is the leader of the party with the most TDs. Ireland also has a president, who is the head of state. The president is elected directly by the people. Presidential candidates must be over 35 years of age. The president represents Ireland at official engagements, but he or she does not run the country. Ireland's Supreme Court decides whether new laws are allowed under the constitution. Judges are appointed by the Taoiseach and his or her cabinet of ministers.

GOVERNMENT		
EXECUTIVE	LEGISLATIVE	JUDICIARY
TAOISEACH	SEANAD ÉIREANN (60 MEMBERS)	SUPREME COURT
CABINET OF MINISTERS	DÁIL ÉIREANN (166 MEMBERS)	HIGH COURT

ENTERING EUROPE

The roots of the European Union (EU) lie in the aftermath of World War II. Nations that had been at war decided to work together. Instead of charging each other to import and export goods across their borders, they formed a "single market." Richer nations also gave money to the poorer ones so that all countries could operate equally.

Ireland joined the EU in 1973. As one of the poorer EU countries at the time, Ireland was given a lot of money. It used it to make farming more productive, to build new roads, and to improve the education system.

▲ The gold stars of the European flag are arranged next to the green, white, and orange of the Irish flag before an EU meeting in Dublin.

European Union was put to the vote in 1972; it was approved. In 2002 the Irish also voted to drop the *punt*—its original currency—and adopt the euro.

As a traditional Catholic country, Ireland has a constitution that enshrines the importance of the family and of marriage. However, family life today is very different from how it was in 1937, when the constitution was adopted. For example, about 30 percent of Irish babies are born to unmarried mothers each year. It was just 5 percent 25 years ago. Also, the constitution made divorce illegal. However, in response to changes in social attitudes, a referendum voted to make divorce legal in 1997.

Taking Care

The constitution also states that the government must look after the welfare of all its people and try to

ensure a basic standard of living for all. The state provides free education, including college. As a result 80 percent of young people have a degree. Healthcare, as with most countries, exists under both a public and private system.

The Celtic Tiger

When Sean Lemass became Taoiseach, or head of government, in 1959, he began the Program for Economic Expansion to modernize the economy. Lemass wanted foreign companies to set up businesses in Ireland. To encourage them, he cut taxes and reformed the education system to ensure that the Irish

TROUBLE IN THE NORTH

When Ireland became the Irish Free State in 1922, six counties remained under British rule as Northern Ireland. But Catholic people in Northern Ireland often felt discriminated against by the Protestants, who were the majority. In the late 1960s, Catholics began a peaceful civil-rights movement. Some also used violence in an attempt to make Northern Ireland part of the Republic. The largest of these armed groups was the Provisional IRA, named after the organization that freed the rest of Ireland in the 1920s. Protestants wanting to remain British also set up "loyalist" units, such as the UVF—Ulster Volunteer Force.

The IRA targeted the British troops sent into towns to keep order. In 1972, British soldiers shot dead 13 unarmed Catholics on a civil-rights march. That day is remembered as Bloody Sunday. For the next 20 years the different groups took part in a cycle of violence known as the Troubles. The IRA also attacked targets in England.

In 1993 the British and Irish governments began to steer the two sides toward peace. In 1998 the Good Friday Agreement was signed, which made Northern Ireland a self-governing part of the United Kingdom. The IRA, UVF, and most other paramilitary organizations have agreed to stop fighting, and divisions in communities are beginning to heal.

▼ A colorful mural in a Catholic area of Belfast, the capital of Northern Ireland, celebrates the 1916 Easter Rising rebellion against British rule.

▲ Computers arrive at the end of the assembly line at a factory in Limerick. The factory is run by a U.S. technology company.

▼ A statue is made from Waterford crystal. This Irish glassware is sold around the world.

workforce would be educated and capable of doing any job. Wages were low in Ireland compared to other parts of Europe, so Ireland's workers were inexpensive but highly skilled.

Eventually the plan began working very well. From 1994 to 2004, the country had the fastest-growing economy in the world. Ireland went from being one of the poorest countries in Europe to the second wealthiest. It was nicknamed the "Celtic Tiger" because its economic growth mirrored that of the "Asian Tigers," South Korea and Taiwan in the 1980s.

American companies were especially interested in Ireland. Irish workers speak English, and they are on the western edge of Europe, just a short flight from North America. Three American computer giants— Microsoft, Intel, and Dell—located their European headquarters in Ireland; many others were to follow.

Modern Manufacturing

Ireland specializes in industries that do not need huge imports of raw materials. They include electronics, pharmaceuticals, and biotechnology, which now contribute 75 percent of the country's total industrial output. Ireland is the world's largest exporter of software. It produces half of all the software sold in

Europe's stores. Currently 13 of the world's largest 15 pharmaceutical companies have factories in Ireland. Six out of ten of the world's top-selling medicines are made there.

Crystal and Cows

Agriculture, which was for so long Ireland's main source of income, has fallen in its economic importance. However, Ireland's largest natural resource is still its high-quality grassland. As a result, its agriculture is based largely on grazing animals, particularly cattle. The country produces huge quantities of milk and other dairy products. Much of this food is sold abroad. For example, Ireland supplies many Middle Eastern countries with beef.

A few other traditional Irish industries remain. Waterford in the south is famous around the world for its fine glassware, known as Waterford crystal. The crystal was first made in the city in 1783 and is now produced on a huge scale.

Crystal items are made by hand and they are found in several famous locations. The chandeliers in England's Windsor Castle are made from Waterford glass, as is the New Year's Eve Ball that is lowered each year in New York City's Times Square. In addition, the winners of the nine annual

INDUSTRY MAP

There is very little heavy industry in Ireland. Among the few sites were huge fertilizer factories in Cork and Wicklow, but these closed down in 2003. Ireland's wealth now comes largely from service industries based in and around the cities. However, Ireland does have a new manufacturing base located in clean, modern factories. They include computer assembly centers and pharmaceutical plants.

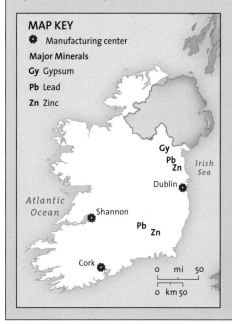

MAP KEY
⚙ Manufacturing center
Major Minerals
Gy Gypsum
Pb Lead
Zn Zinc

Gy
Pb
Zn
Irish Sea
Dublin ⚙

Atlantic Ocean
Shannon ⚙
Pb
Zn

Cork ⚙

0   mi   50

0   km 50

MADAM PRESIDENT

Mary Robinson was elected as Ireland's first female president in 1990. After a decade of violence in the north of Ireland and high unemployment in the republic that led thousands to leave to make a life abroad, Robinson's election was a turning point. With her, the Irish were voting for someone who stood for fairness and tolerance.

Robinson served the full seven years of the Irish presidential term and was an important figure during a period of great change. After her presidency, Robinson became the United Nations High Commissioner for Human Rights. The election of the next president in 1997 was dominated by women candidates, and Robinson was succeeded by Mary McAleese.

▲ **Mary Robinson casts her vote in a referendum on Ireland's place in the EU.**

Masters' Series tennis tournaments are awarded with trophies cut from Waterford crystal.

Another famous Irish export is Guinness, a thick beer that is made from barley and is almost pitch black. Pouring a glass of Guinness properly is a skilled job; it is not a drink for the thirsty because the full process takes a little time.

▼ **Despite the great advances in the Irish economy in recent years, much of its land is still devoted to traditional farming.**

Land of Legends

A glass of Guinness is just one attraction for tourists on vacation in Ireland. Others come to enjoy the amazing green landscapes littered with historic monuments. Tourism is an important Irish industry.

It employs over 100,000 people, who look after 6 million foreign visitors every year.

Dublin is one of the most popular destinations in the world for short or weekend breaks. People come for "the *craic*," the Irish phrase for "good fun." Many American visitors like to trace their family history in the country.

Challenges and Opportunities

Ireland's booming economy has created 30,000 new millionaires, but wealth has not always translated into better living conditions for all. Many communities are still poor, and crime is on the increase. The new wealth has widened the gap between the rich and the poor. The population is rising, so facilities such as roads, hospitals, and schools are now stretched to their limits. They were once paid for with grants from the European Union (EU). Now that Ireland is rich, it must use its own money to maintain them.

Ireland faces the future with mixed moods. It is confident after years of being a relatively poor country on the edge of Europe, but the Irish are also concerned about what other changes their future will bring.

▲ Dublin's Grafton Street is crowded with people. Dublin is regarded as one of Europe's most fun cities.

▼ A bus brings tourists to the Rock of Cashel, a 1,000-year-old castle and church in Tipperary.

Add a Little Extra to Your Country Report!

I f you are assigned to write a report about Ireland, you'll want to include basic information about the country, of course. The Fast Facts chart on page 8 will give you a good start. The rest of the book will give you the details you need to create a full and up-to-date paper or PowerPoint presentation. But what can you do to make your report more fun than anyone else's? If you use your imagination and dig a bit deeper into some of the topics introduced in this book, you're sure to come up with information that will make your report unique!

>Flag

Perhaps you could explain the history of Ireland's flag, and the meanings of its colors. Go to **www.crwflags.com/fotw/flags** for more information.

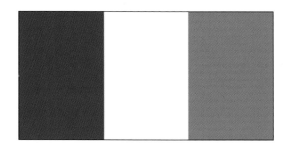

>National Anthem

How about downloading Ireland's national anthem, and playing it for your class? At **www.nationalanthems.info** you'll find what you need, including the words to the anthem, plus sheet music it. Simply pick "I" and then "Ireland" from the list on the left-hand side of the screen, and you're on your way.

>Time Difference

If you want to understand the time difference between Ireland and where you are, this Web site can help: **www.worldtimeserver.com**. Just pick "Ireland" from the list on the left. If you called someone in Ireland right now, would you wake them up from their sleep?

>Currency

Another Web site will convert your money into euros, the currency used in Ireland. You'll want to know how much money to bring if you're ever lucky enough to travel to Ireland: **www.xe.com/ucc**.

>Weather

Why not check the current weather in Ireland? It's easy—go to **www.weather.com** to find out if it's sunny or cloudy, warm or cold in Ireland right now! Pick "World" from the headings at the top of the page. Then search for Ireland. Click on any city. Be sure to click on the tabs below the weather report for Sunrise/Sunset information, Weather Watch, and Business Travel Outlook, too. Scroll down the page for the 36-hour Forecast and a satellite weather map. Compare your weather to the weather in the Irish city you chose. Is this a good season, weather-wise, for a person to travel to Ireland?

>Miscellaneous

Still want more information? Simply go to National Geographic's World Atlas for Young Explorers at **http://www.nationalgeographic.com/ kids-world.atlas**. It will help you find maps, photos, music, games, and other features that you can use to jazz up your report.

Glossary

Banished to be sent away from a place forever.

Climate the average weather of a certain place at different times of year.

Communism a system of government where a single political party rules a country with the job of ensuring that wealth is shared equally among all the people in the country.

Conservation protecting plants and animals that are becoming rare.

Culture a collection of beliefs, traditions, and styles that belongs to people living in a certain part of the world.

Democracy a government chosen by all its people through elections.

Economy the system by which a country creates wealth through making and trading in products.

Exported transported and sold outside the country of origin.

Famine a period when there is not enough food, everyone is hungry, and many people die from starvation.

Fertile somewhere that is very good for growing plants.

Fungus a type of living thing that produces mushrooms and molds.

Glacier a body of ice formed over thousands of years, mainly by layers of snow, that slowly flows on land.

Hedgerow a series of bushes that are grown into a boundary between fields.

Imported brought into the country from abroad.

Mythology a collection of stories, often a mixture of facts and legend, that tells the history of a nation or people.

Natural resources naturally occurring materials and substances that can be collected and sold, such as oil, metals, or lumber.

Neolithic from the New Stone Age period, when people used stones to make tools and large buildings.

Patron saint a country's main saint.

Plateau an area of land that is high but flat.

Prehistoric from a time before any history was recorded.

Protestant a Christian who belongs to one of several churches that broke away from the Catholic Church in the 16th century.

Raw materials the basic items needed to make a product; factories turn raw materials into manufactured goods.

Republic a country that is ruled by an elected head of state, such as a president.

Roman Catholic a Christian who follows a branch of the religion based in Rome, Italy.

Scandinavia a region of northwestern Europe, which includes Norway, Sweden, and Denmark. Iceland and Finland may also be included.

Scribe a person who writes things down; in the past scribes were usually monks and were the only people who could write.

Tetrapod a four-legged animal.

Bibliography

Olson, Kay Melchisedech. *Ireland*. Mankato, MN: Blue Earth Books, 2004.

Sasek, M. *This is Ireland*. New York, NY: Universe, 2005.

http://www.historyireland.com/ (historical information from *History Ireland* magazine)

http://www.irlgov.ie/ (official Web site of the Irish Government)

http://www.ireland-information.com/irelandmaps.htm (detailed maps of Ireland)

Further Information

National Geographic Articles

Lange, Karen E. "Tales from the Bog." NATIONAL GEOGRAPHIC (September 2007): 80-93.

Web sites to explore

More fast facts about Ireland, from the CIA (Central Intelligence Agency): https://www.cia.gov/library/publications/the-world-fact-book/geos/ei.html

Ireland has some of the largest castles in the world. Some are ancient ruins while others are still working buildings. Find out more about them and see pictures at: http://www.ireland-now.com/castles.html This site also has lots of other information about everything from mythology to favorite Irish recipes, including the famous Irish stews.

See, hear

There are many ways to get a taste of life in Ireland, such as movies and music. You might be able to locate these:

Live Ireland Radio
Listen to music broadcast from Ireland 24 hours a day. There is a channel for traditional Irish folk music and one for pop tunes. A third channel carries talk radio with comedy, interviews and other features. Have a listen at http://www.liveireland.com/live.shtml There is even a webcam showing the Dublin street where the station is based so you can watch what's happening right now.

Artemis Fowl
Get into the mind of Artemis Fowl, the master criminal of Ireland's fairy land created by author Eoin Colfer, by playing

this code-breaking game http://www.artemisfowl.com/game/pop_up/

RTE Young Peoples
Watch some video clips and full TV programs made for Irish children. The Den is for younger viewers, while TTV is aimed at teenagers.

Waking Ned Devine (1998)
A family film set in a tiny Irish village, which celebrates the funny side of rural Irish life. When Ned Devine wins a huge cash prize in the Irish lottery, he dies of shock. The rest of the villagers have to work together—and fast—to claim the money without the lottery organizers finding out that the winner has actually passed on.

Index

Credits

Picture Credits

Front Cover – Spine: R de Man/Shutterstock; Top: Richard Nowitz/NGIC; Low Far Left: Martin Gray/NGIC; Low Left: Cotton Coulson/NGIC; Low Right: Nicolas Reynard /NGIC; Low Far Right: Brian J. Skerry/NGIC.

Interior – Corbis: Bettmann: 28 lo; Jonathan Blair: 20 up; Gary Cook/Robert Harding World Imagery: 33 up; Richard Cummins: 36 lo; Kathy De Witt/Lebrecht Music & Arts: 38 lo; Farrell Grehan: 48 center; Yves Herman/Reuters: 51 up; Karen Hunnt: 38 up; Robbie Jack: 42 up; Bob Krist: 16 lo; Alan Lewis/Sygma: 50 up; Barry Lewis: TP, 41 up; Alan MacWeeney: 20 lo; Paul Mcerlane/epa: 53 lo; Gideon Mendel: 3 right, 56-57, 54 up, 57 up; Richard Nowitz: 29 lo, 54 lo; Matthew Polak/Sygma: 40 up, 56 up; Susie Posst Rust: 2 right, 14-15, 45 up, 56 lo; Michael St. Maur Sheil: 44 lo; Stringer: 3 left, 34-35; Stringer/AFP: 28 up; Gary Sweeney: 13 lo; The Irish Image Collection: 5 up, 13 up, 30 up, 57 lo; Tim Thompson: 34-35, 45 lo, 52 up; Felix Zaska: 31 lo; Getty Images: Tim Boyle: 32 up; M. J. Kim: 43 up; Jerry Young/Dorling Kindersley: 21 lo; NGIC: Sam Abell: 11 up, 42 lo, Robert Clark: 26 lo; Cotton Coulson: 10 up; Nicole Duplaix: 19 lo; Martin Gray: 24 up, 27 lo, 27 up; Gail Mooney: 2 left, 6-7; Chris Rainer: 21 up, 42 lo; Jim Richardson: 2-3, 10 lo, 12 up, 22-23, 39 up; Medford Taylor: 18 up; Shutterstock: Peter Dankow: 59 up.

For more information, please call 1-800-NGS-LINE (647-5463) or write to the following address:

NATIONAL GEOGRAPHIC SOCIETY
1145 17th Street N.W.
Washington, D.C. 20036-4688 U.S.A.

Visit us online at www.nationalgeographic.com/books

Library of Congress Cataloging-in-Publication Data available on request
ISBN: 978-1-4263-0299-2

Printed in the United States of America

Series design by Jim Hiscott.

Front Cover—Top: A bookstore on Harry Street, Dublin; Low Far Left: Detail of a Celtic cross; Low Left: Halfpenny Bridge spans the Liffey River in Dublin; Low Right: A boy holds his horse in Ballymun, County Dublin; Low Far Right: Cliffs on the coast of Kerry

Page 1—Schoolchildren on Tory Island, Donegal; Icon image on spine, Contents page, and throughout: Shamrock

Produced through the worldwide resources of the National Geographic Society

John M. Fahey, Jr., *President and Chief Executive Officer;* Gilbert M. Grosvenor, *Chairman of the Board;* Tim T. Kelly, *President,* Global Media Group; John Q. Griffin, *President, Publishing;* Nina D. Hoffman, *Executive Vice President, President of Book Publishing Group*

National Geographic Staff for this Book

Nancy Laties Feresten, *Vice President, Editor-in-Chief of Children's Books*
Bea Jackson, *Director of Design and Illustration*
Jim Hiscott, *Art Director*
Virginia Koeth, *Project Editor*
Lori Epstein, *Illustrations Editor*
Stacy Gold, Nadia Hughes, *Illustrations Research Editors*
R. Gary Colbert, *Production Director*
Lewis R. Bassford, *Production Manager*
Grace Hill, *Associate Managing Editor*
Rachel Faulise, Nicole Elliott, *Manufacturing Managers*
Maps, *Mapping Specialists, Ltd.*

Brown Reference Group plc. Staff for this Book

Volume Editor: Tom Jackson
Designer: Dave Allen
Picture Manager: Clare Newman
Maps: Martin Darlison
Artwork: Darren Awuah
Index: Kay Ollerenshaw
Senior Managing Editor: Tim Cooke
Children's Publisher: Anne O'Daly
Editorial Director: Lindsey Lowe

About the Authors

ANNA MCQUINN was born and grew up in Ireland, studying English and history at University College, Cork. She took a post-graduate education course and taught for a number of years before emigrating to the UK to work in children's publishing.

COLM MCQUINN was born and grew up in Ireland. He studied history and archaeology at University College, Cork. After teaching in Europe, he returned to Ireland and qualified as an archivist. He is currently in charge of Dublin's county archives.

About the Consultants

ELIZABETH MALCOLM is Gerry Higgins Professor of Irish Studies at the University of Melbourne, Australia. Her research focuses on modern Irish social history, especially violence, gender, medicine and migration. Her latest book is *The Irish Policeman, 1822-1922: A Life* (2006). Professor Malcolm, who taught for many years in Ireland and England, is a Fellow of the Royal Historical Society and of the Academy of Social Sciences in Australia.

JOHN MCDONAGH is a lecturer in the geography department at the National University of Ireland, Galway. John's current research interests focus on rural development, sustainable environments, rural transport, and mobility. He has been involved in a number of European-funded research projects and is the author of *Renegotiating Rural Development in Ireland* (2001). He is currently completing a co-edited volume entitled *A Living Countryside: The Politics of Sustainable Development in Rural Ireland* (2008).

Time Line of
Irish History

B.C.

ca 6000 The first people cross the land bridge from Scotland and settle Ireland.

ca 3200 Passage tombs are built in the Boyne Valley.

ca 1800 Metalworking begins in Ireland.

ca 700 The Celts arrive in Ireland.

A.D.

ca 432 Saint Patrick arrives in Ireland and converts much of the country to Christianity.

795 The first Norsemen land on the coast of Lambay, an island near Dublin, and establish a Norse settlement.

ca. 800 The Book of Kells is created, perhaps at the Irish monastery at Iona. This illuminated manuscript is an Irish masterpiece of incredible design complexity.

1000

1014 The Irish king Brian Boru unites the country to defeat the Vikings at the Battle of Clontarf, but dies soon after the battle.

1170 The Norman invasion of Ireland begins with the arrival of "Strongbow," the Earl of Pembroke. A year later he becomes king of Leinster.

1171 King Henry II takes control of a large part of Ireland.

1366 The Statutes of Kilkenny are passed by the English to limit the power of Norman settlers in Ireland.

1494 Henry VII makes Irish parliaments subject to the English Privy Council and brings Ireland further under English control.

1600

1601 Forces sent by Queen Elizabeth I defeat Hugh O'Neill, the Earl of Tyrone, and his allies at the Battle of Kinsale.

1603 The English conquer the whole of Ireland.

1641 After years of Protestant English settlement in Ireland, Catholic Irish riot for the return of their land and kill hundreds of Protestants.

1649 England's lord protector Oliver Cromwell arrives in Ireland. His troops kill thousands at Drogheda and Wexford. Cromwell hands Catholic Irish land to Protestant settlers.

1690 William of Orange defeats James II's troops at the Battle of Boyne and defends the Protestant community in Northern Ireland.

1700

1782 The Irish Parliament gains the power to make its own laws.

1798 The Society of United Irishmen and other groups rebel in an attempt to achieve Irish independence. Tens of thousands die in failed rising.

1800

1801 The Act of Union formally joins Ireland and Britain to create the Kingdom of Great Britain and Ireland.